SCREAM / QUEEN

SCREAM

/QUEEN

POEMS

CD ESKILSON

CINCINNATI 2025

Acre Books is made possible by the support of the Robert and Adele Schiff Foundation and the Department of English at the University of Cincinnati.

Copyright © 2025 by CD Eskilson
All rights reserved
Printed in the United States of America

ISBN-13 (pbk) 978-1-946724-87-8
ISBN-13 (ebook) 978-1-946724-88-5

Designed by Barbara Neely Bourgoyne
Cover art: iStock/Vizerskaya

No part of this work may be reproduced or transmitted in any form or by any means, electronic or mechanical, including photocopying and recording, or by any information storage or retrieval system, without express written permission, except in the case of brief quotations embodied in critical articles and reviews.

Epigraph: Billy-Ray Belcourt, excerpt from "Grief after Grief after Grief after Grief" from *This Wound Is a World*. Copyright © 2017, 2019 by Billy-Ray Belcourt. Originally published in 2017 by Frontenac House. Published by the University of Minnesota Press, 2019. Used with the permission of the author, Frontenac House, and the University of Minnesota Press. All rights reserved.

Chen Chen, excerpt from "Race to the Tree" from *When I Grow Up I Want to Be a List of Further Possibilities*. Copyright © 2017 by Chen Chen. Used with the permission of The Permissions Company, LLC, on behalf of BOA Editions, Ltd., boaeditions.org.

The press is based at the University of Cincinnati, Department of English, Arts & Sciences Hall, Room 248, PO Box 210069, Cincinnati, OH, 45221-0069.

Acre Books titles may be purchased at a discount for educational use. For information please email business@acre-books.com.

CONTENTS

FOUND / FOOTAGE

King Ghidorah / 3
On Witchcraft / 5
What Starts as a List Poem about OCD / 7
Palos Verdes / 9
Burning Haibun for Geryon / 10
How Are They Picking the Next *Halloween* Director? / 12
After I Fail to Come Out Again, the Apparition Comes / 13
Update on HIM from *Powerpuff Girls* / 14

BODY / HORROR

Recipe for Roasted Broccoli / 17
A Brief History of Broken Glass / 18
Dystychiphobia, or Fear of Accidents / 20
Heredity / 22
Ghost Story with My Uncle / 23
Portrait with Inconclusive Lab Results / 24
When People Tell You GAD Can't Be That Bad / 25
Deleted Scene: Each Time I'm Trans Enough / 26
Confession from Medusa's Head / 29
During Intro to Film Theory / 31
At the Midnight Show of *Sleepaway Camp* / 32

JUMP / SCARE

Prey: A Gloss / 35
Trans Panic Contrapuntal / 39

Fan Mail for the Headless Horseman / 40
Be My Baby / 41
I Séance with My Uncle at MacArthur Park / 44
Finsta of Icarus in Drag / 45
Accidental Selfie in the Photo of a Window Quote / 46
My Roommate Buffalo Bill / 47

PARA / NORMAL

I Still Haven't Seen *The Fly* / 51
How to Be Happy / 52
Hollywood Forever Cemetery / 54
The Demon King Paimon Comes By for Monstera Clippings / 55
Arkansas Bans Healthcare for Trans Youth / 57
Transcestor Creation Myth / 58
The Ocean Within Me / 59
Every Man Their Mortal Enemy, Every Woman's Beauty Prey / 62

SUPER / NATURAL

Our Family Leaves the Haunted House / 65
When Meryl Streep Sings "Dancing Queen" in *Mamma Mia!* / 66
Portrait as Werewolf / 67
What I Will Write about My Father / 68
Since Moving from the Beach / 69
Reversed House Cleansing / 70
Ode to an Anti-Joke / 71
Draft Message to My Sibling after Top Surgery / 73

Notes / 75
Acknowledgments / 77

Haunting is a gender. Gender is another word for horror story.

—BILLY-RAY BELCOURT

FOUND / FOOTAGE

King Ghidorah

I don't know surviving to a sequel
or how to speak about anxiety outside disaster.

I've perfected shrieking onlooker,
the dodge and weave of plans and scramble
      over sentences. I've refuged in the
ribbit of a push-lock or a pill cap

      though no one tells you this anticipation
files fangs, buds another head on the gargantuan.

Picture a hydra squirming from my lips,
yawned wings knocked against the sun, its belly
filled with burned worlds bowing, over.

Before we watch *Godzilla* you explain that
King Ghidorah crash-lands here from outer space
to decimate humanity

      but all I see's my hand, its fingers serpenting,
its lightning tips that scar a typhooned sky.

One scene from the movie I recall's
a father helping children stack the rubble
      into play forts, crawl inside
          the avalanching walls—

how they don't seek protection in the wreck
but a proximity to ruins,
      the dragon scales that
drop as shingles above their heads.

I wonder how I've begged for this destruction,
the gravity of every panic beamed against
      my chest that leaves me in a writhe;

I ponder how inheritance comes in many forms,
one of them the jagged spines I've palmed.

      How a friend once stole my medication
just to see how many heads I'd scream.

      I want to behemoth, be the biggest
violence in the galaxy, smite fear and death.

What I mean is that I want to wield
a smoldered city, have its demolition
be anything I dream:

      my memory of prey
gone ruthless, stormblack wings,
my learning how to roar.

On Witchcraft

Statues of Hecate show a triple-headed goddess. A being far too myriad for just one mouth. There's a longing for what's lost in shrines, engraved into a frieze. What's held inside a myth.

My sibling knew defiance early on. Their buzz cuts, constant binder. New name at the bank and license photo. F. walks through forests, filling clearings with their beard. Shows how to curse a compromise, pull the moon down with both hands.

Just how enclosures took the peasantry from commons, witch-hunts took the women from their bodies, I glean from Federici. I want to be the open field and commune. The strength that would provide. To coven in a word like *them* and reclaim multitude as gender.

In cinema: *The VVitch* ends as stubbled sisters levitate through pines, their chorus claiming night. I order my capri pants, scroll through rows of summer dresses. Text photos to a friend and hope to find my sabbath field. Reach out from disenchantment still unsure of what to grasp.

I scour terms for remedy that also can mean poison. Land on *pharmakon*. The possibility F. shows me, though how little feels like mine. My chest beneath the pressing stones. A Pride event where people call me *little F.*, so quickly lose my name. The rock soon disappears me.

Each horror movie archives a resistance. *The Autopsy of Jane Doe* shows how a body won't be dominated. Skull-split, drained, and still won't open. Her hexes pry mortician's skin. I study and take notes.

Is this dysphoria revolt or just reaction? My ankles chafe on ducking stool. I stalk beaches, pockets lined with gold and lead. Draw shapes in the sand to summon what's *enough*. Fix my lipstick, bury men, stretch my spine into the sky. I conjure what I can't contain.

What Starts as a List Poem about OCD

- becomes sliced apple on a toothpick
      tossed into the ocean;

- or pill bugs tacked to billboards
      meant to wriggle punctuation;

- I pin my definitions of *to be*
      for further scientific study;

- because my usage rhymes with
      push-locks in a bathroom;

- because it's too predictable to mention
      locks when writing on obsession;

- in *Obsession*, a man apologizes for the wait
      time at a restaurant till his wife explodes;

- till her body's bits of paper
      flurry down like snow;

- the scene remains a dream
      for everyone except the man;

- in a dream, a vulture perches on my
      chest and I stroke it while it feasts;

- its bald head nestles in my arm
      as I stack roadkill bones in columns;

- in *Obsession,* the man can't stop erecting
      bollards to prevent his late wife's death;

- he can't stop waking as a tree
      that's felled to feed a blaze;

- I can't stop saying *sorry* is my
    name, the start to every question;

- with *say*, mean something whipped
    across the small of a back;

- the search for what's lodged
    between a blood-jet and disaster;

Palos Verdes

Limpets clung to rocks way out
where we waded at low tide,
tried not to flatten sand crabs
seeking shelter like we did. The cliff

where we would wait at high tide
when the tourists roamed, took shells,
seeking treasure like we did. The cliff
passed red and purple, sunstreaks low.

When the tourists left, pretense took off:
we fumbled in the sand, ditched belts,
passed red and purple marks down chests.
Nobody knew. Dark came, the car lights flashed,

we fumbled in the sand to cover flesh.
Still green to taking dick then, I hoped
nobody knew you came. The car ride after,
tried not to flatten down so small.

Burning Haibun for Geryon

Night quiets in his ruby look. Night dispersed as snowmelt, his wings stretched in mock flight. A soughing stretches between pines. Here he recalls the chime-like startle. Recalls he's a boy who aches with what's owed. His throat recalls pruned orchids, something earned with excise. Clipping the red curls off himself. He overwrites the reasons for his body to endure till finding a defense, a shield just like the T-shirt some other boy gave him once. Who cut wingholes in its back, hung the scraps to nightghost through his sleep. In truth, that boy cut wingholes to escape him. This night cut into prism, peaked at quiet. He regards his monsterhood: the lips that cloak his fangs, his birth dropped from a dragon, life a violated sky. He conjures up another lover to abandon him at how he chokes on want. Flightwreck unfolds inside his skull. He thinks of where else he might come from, shade unyoking from his body. The wall of night collapses as he slips into its mouth.

//

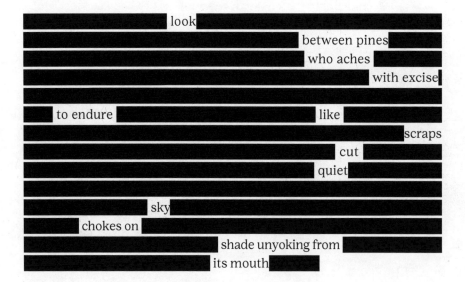

//

A soughing ████████████████████████ startle ███████████ boy ██ aches ████████████████ recalls pruned orchids ███████████████ Clipping █████ off ███████████████ his ██████████ he █████

How Are They Picking the Next *Halloween* Director?

Because your CV's filled with brilliant acts
of hiding, reemerging, disappearing on yourself.
Speed-walking in a straight line, trying to be
undeterred. Next, you're terrifying others:
your coming out's a jump scare, shrieks when
pulling off the mask. You've got experience
with striking fear as an idea, a shape prowling
through reactionary minds. Who claim
you trail them home with the trans agenda
when you just live in the same building.

You're good at guiding actors since you're
subtle, so much your horror isn't known to you.
Followed at the store again by some faux
final girl and still you haven't said a word.
Your expertise is *lurking* parks and streets,
not that you have a right to walk here too,
to wear a jumpsuit flattering your hips.
An audience tries spotting you in every
frame. You'd tagline the installment:
What happens when we leave her be?

After I Fail to Come Out Again, the Apparition Comes

want to love / her accident / her teeth chipped on my name / her body's quaking fidget / tossing witchbones in the cinder / at night we sleep / we wink / we razor-slick the ceiling / board a crossfixed longing / creased with heat / at night she smears my lips / till wincing / till I thock We off the tongue / smithereen our séance / desiccate the sanctuary / because she won't dimlight in me any longer / won't blankspace or burrow / down a bed / her protest is a jay's wing / jabbed into my jaw / here the violence spreads / here its virulent velocity / the violet bruisepush / left my skin / left clawed / left tattooed with her mark / indelible / enduring /

Update on HIM from *Powerpuff Girls*

Of course I fangirled seeing HIM work
at a coffee shop on Wilshire. Can't say I wasn't
gawking at this misfit Mephistopheles, this idol
of my odd-duck childhood. Their pink tulle
scrunched beneath a khaki apron, thigh-highs
swapped for tennis shoes. I tried to play it cool
in line but HIM kept chipping mugs and flubbing
orders, popped an oatmilk carton with their claw.
People snickered, mimicked their falsetto walking
to the sugar station. HIM reminded me of me: of something
queer and clumsy that attracted too much notice. A target
on two fronts. Reminded me of guessing what the joke's
about and making it a game. HIM's beard poked through
the hairnet that they wore. They shattered someone's
lemonade and shards rained on the ground. I wanted
to help, fetch oven mitts, but thought this might be patronizing.
Wanted to repay their showing me to layer crimson, strut
maniacally, craft gender out of points and curves. I feared
distracting them. HIM spilled espresso on the bar
that got on someone's pants. They kept apologizing,
same as when I asked my boss to use my new name
and he wouldn't. The *sorry* added to my hands. I tried to
make it easy for them by getting bottled juice. Tried not
to stare, made small talk about muffins, which worked until
I almost walked off without paying. HIM laughed
at least. Each time I went back I hoped to see them there
but never did. I hoped HIM wasn't fired. I swear I saw
them once while backing out my car: a black North Face
above an apron, salmon ruffle peeking out. That's enough
for me to know, I think—it's enough to know they're there.

BODY / HORROR

Recipe for Roasted Broccoli

When my sibling says they don't feel subject to our father's mental illness I focus on cleaving through the broccoli stalks. Separating florets from the trunk, dousing them in salt and olive oil. I want to question the stem severed from its leaves but this thread tangles when I start tossing with my hands. My sibling postulates how ordinary growing up was, how little we'd known about what's heritable until later. Until trying to form relationships and being *too much* every time. How our narratives eschew slipping grips and siren wails, my sibling says. I watch my broccoli in the oven as I nod, try to toss the stripped green artery into the kitchen trash. I miss and hit the wall. I want a gesture that can prove them right. I want to glue the front door lock our father drove back to review every morning before work. To sand the floorboard his obsession tried to level. Last month, I tried cleansing *sorry* from my language but didn't last the afternoon. I tried until it rained and knew whose fault it was. I know our father would've folded long before me: would've blamed himself for gravity, would've safety-pinned the drops back on the clouds.

A Brief History of Broken Glass

Capri Sun pouch at college parties
Ocean Spray at bars
for every birthday   declining drinks
an impulse cocked and ready
    in the throat

                         I'm dried blood after cracking a new
                               wine stem, dull rust linger
                        after Swiffer wipes and shadows
                                      stagger out

family history prompts dry
pause at the kickback   try speaking
spirits into fuel, sharing visions
    of slurred wreckage

                      I'm fourth shot dropped on weeknights
                      and a problem calling quits, denial
                      of drowning but still urging that
                              it's better not to start

at brunch friends
order rosemary greyhounds
    recall front planters
back home   back then
hoping to perfume
on air   escape inside

                        I'm cracked pipe stashed by Uncle
                        into pockets, tongued to keep on
                           burning, keep on beaming
                                dime-bright smiles

inside   nestfuls of failed rosary,
chipped crosses off another
uncle's drawer   here Christ
dies next to a bad license

                                      I'm bottle factory that swallowed up
                                                Great-Grandpa's arm, him
                                      bringing work home by the case,
                              the sharded skin Gram patched in quiet

the basement filled with photos
crammed in waterlogged and cracking
frames   names floating through
   the dark keep swimming

                                                    I'm looking in the mirror
                                                          only long enough
                                                              to throw a stone

Dystychiphobia, or Fear of Accidents

My father flies into the windshield
as a baby, a bloody smear
that never speaks.

      Rather, it's the future that
his mother sees when she's rear-ended
at the grocery store. She grips him

like a pail and scoops beach sand
down his throat. Spades fear
to form his bones. He teaches me

to drive with fingers kinked across
a lap, fried nerves scrambling for release.

::

I crouch inside my mother and do nothing
as we tumble through dune grass:

her back snaketwists to keep the car door
off me, arms tatter into ancient scrolls.

At birth I brace for impact
and splay my legs into an axle.

::

In 2002, a morning fog engulfs
the freeway: two hundred cars
collide into a fishkill. Passengers

stuck captive behind fanged glass
while metal shrieks, oil ribbons
out in streams.

Years later my sibling sits
here as a plum tossed on the roadside.

As a child, I would crawl into
their bed, my body rolling over theirs—

again they tense and shoulder weight
and try to keep themselves from tearing.

::

Dropped stone plummets through
the surf, the coastline sieged by sea.

I haven't found a proper way
to crash yet—

      to plunge into a grinning wave,
        to plunge like knife and pluck at thread
and feel lineage unraveling. Dashboard

stops the plummet of my skull, my wreckage
scattered through the ripples—

I linger like a closed mouth in the driveway
and will do anything to move.

Heredity

Nobody told the stories as they happened:
        every blood dance, panic pulling bodies

past the chorus of a prayer. Omitted how
        each relative unraveled without respool.

Alone I've traced the wires inside walls
        out through the fields, found a lunatic

substation. Found Uncle smashing taillights, Grandma
        traipsing through ERs. Learned what current

frenzies blood. Nobody told me knowing
        would do little—I'd still end up a house falling.

Ghost Story with My Uncle

      Boy-ghost hunts for sweetness,
soon finds stubble raking hips
          in smokeblue swells of back seats.

      Wailing starts without a sound,
an afterlife on knees behind the gym.
          His legend soon spreads.

      Boy-ghost meets shoulder bump
and bruising stare, cracked windshield
          in the parking lot. His parents

      find the thrift-store heels, shriek
and curse possession. Call in counselors
          to shoo locusts down his throat

      and gnaw him see-through. Boy-ghost
learns raging silence, how to drown it
          like his grandpa did in glasses.

      Boy-ghost whites with powder,
deadhard body like a tomb. Caught punching
          out the window of a drag club

      he would go to, his teeth scattered
by police. Friends scatter from his moan.
          Boy-ghost wishing he was mist,

      a cloud left floating below moon:
something shapeless others pass through
          and will never try to hold.

Portrait with Inconclusive Lab Results

I name it with an image:
an orchard where the black plums
tilt and shake, shudder
aubades to their boughs, then fall.

I wait below to catch what drops,
unwelt the maim of skin. I siphon
violence from flesh and tongue
the sweetblood for a name. Tongue

the ulcer in my cheek, taste the sour
in my stomach. Trace disease's lineage.

I'd like to think there's something solid
in the sign we mark a virus with—
that garbled printouts and graphs grant
full bones to the ghost. Give an enemy to lash.

My doctor offers dim fluorescent, a salt flat
of linoleum. A voice reserved for things with fur.
I stall into my chest while gripped by apparition.

Continue the pill regimen, wince
and house their plummet. Wait and see,
stay haunted. My mouth fills with half-light,
a wreck escaping words. There's *ecstasy*

in this undoing—not the definition's joy but
inundation, overwhelming. Being spirited away.

I can't stay the gravity against this fruit, how
flesh splits from stone. Reaching up, the juice
glints violet through my hand, a sigil I can take.

When People Tell You GAD Can't Be That Bad

imagine sweet alyssum
blanketing the ground[1]

the heaven-scented blooms
like clouds to the cicadas[2]

you move from forest's edge
to cross the meadow, creep[3]

with footsteps slight & nearly
still while wind glides through[4]

to make these petals
sway in the field[5]

---

1. where you grip gravel / drip out rubies / face crammed in the shattered earth / face crammed in a pillow / here where everything will spark / you drip with turpentine / heat-veined autonomic being / here a mouth singed / opened wide / still cannot gasp /

2. crawling over skin with twiggy legs / each stamping down a diagram of shame / its scrawled dimensions / feeling like dried aster down a shirt / an empty bottle / man's breath in an ear / you think of how small you could shrink / how little stays yours through this swarm /

3. & slink & call this your escaping episode / a space between missed calls & texts / not opening the blinds / one image of fatigue's your finger clawing / double bass strings / here see the bone worn with abrasion / here see a body filed down /

4. the quarries mined for sertraline / fluoxetine / citalopram / the quarries mined to pave a synapse / pair the thirsted nerves uprooted / twisted into knotted braids / your knotted hands when trying a half dosage / how each rock drops / lands back at the start /

5. against your skin & offer palimpsest / which tears itself again / anointed in this frenzy / here with no bridge left to cross / here where everything repeats /

Deleted Scene: Each Time I'm Trans Enough

The universe inside my breath
I hold in walking home
the eyes glued to me become planets
my head must be a sun   my dress deep space

my learning to feel small
despite this body's gravity

                not   real

                        but   tries

      to be   a   Star

  be born   be made

                                    a thousand times

    ice

   violence
       or   pathology

but _____

                   not _____
   real _____

                        thinks _____

                  thinks

once loved a good debate with friends
our nostrils flared like telescopes
not these arguments about my name
who knows me more than I do

                                        not   real

           not   real

but   terrifying   very close

             but   criminal

criminal

                             identity

what
                thinks   is

                                    thinks
                           tries
thinks

passing by the squad car
with its officers agape
I taste asteroid out of instinct

                         not   real
not   real

                                     but   tries to be

         not   real

                                        not   real
                    but   _____

                                catch   _____
catch
                                    tries to be
            catch

        tries to   be
                                        catch   tries

Confession from Medusa's Head

Coming to in pangs
and cicatrix, an absence
without end. Zoloft

on the tongue
dissolved while eyes
adjust to burlap's dark.

Lips gum the myth
that I'm left trauma,
twitch and trigger,

these braids hung limp
and venom-dry. A fury
wracks the teeth that

gnash this bag. I seethe
but still can't afterward
this hacking. Can't coax

Pegasus from a neck
wound, gape my trachea,
birth vengeance. I haven't

tried men since, still
feel him pull my hair
to wield me, become

weapon. My fang
that tries to gore
his hand splits

a lover's skin instead.
Remind me how to want
before cracked jaw

or dragon scales. Before
ceramic smashed on temple
floor, inside an ICU. Now

I'm a stare that shards
each boy. Now each broad-
necked warrior believes

my safety's an attack, draws
villainess from terror. Dropped,
I thud like an anchor

tossed in marsh, a burial.
A skull dragged down
by all that it can't vessel.

During Intro to Film Theory

I learned practical effects lend authenticity
to horror, heighten audience immersion. That
death is a deceptive angle and manipulated

prop. Take Glen's demise in *A Nightmare
on Elm Street*: his body swallowed by a bed
and returned as geysered rouge. Filmed

upside-down, the killing defies logic
so we can't look away. In *Alien*, a bursting
creature makes such easy work of ribs.

To shoot: a rubber torso packed with meat.
It's ironic an illusion employed slaughter:
there's so much harm silenced, so much

cruelty made quiet. These bills that flood
statehouses banning bodies, stripping
coverage, cutting lifelines for trans youth

while how little others talk about the gore.
Each day presents a jump scare, hoping
it might bury us, though this violence

started long before. What angle could I
film from to grip an audience and capture
all the care inequities? Without red dye,

people shrug, stay unfazed by our loss.
I chafe against a want for what is owed:
a movie in soft focus with warm colors,

perfect lighting, every scream queen
flagrant with her brilliant smile. Not simply
a new ending, an entirely new script.

At the Midnight Show of *Sleepaway Camp*

My queers and I clear from the aisles annoyed
and damning the director, entering full takedown
mode. A trans girl romps through teens'
dark cabins, the panicked cry of *She's a boy!*

to give this slasher its shock-twist. Today
the image we're all killers remains deadly,
has only grown more mainstream. But others
in our group push back, defend the film.

All huddled at a Denny's, we listen to them
fawn over the catharsis in a murder-fest.
Admit over plates of fries to dreams
of wasting bullies, dropping angry beehives

on assholes throwing slurs. From the ruckus
of debate between our booths, the film's
subversion sharpens: critiques of gendered
violence, forced dysphoria emerge. Can't we

hold both readings of the movie to be true?
Know there's risk in our vindictive gore
but that it offers a resistance. That we might
carry on with movie nights and diner talks,

the uneventful lot of it, an arrow pointed
at the next abuser's throat. Can't we
promise to slay whoever creeps these
woods and return after to the quiet trees?

JUMP / SCARE

Prey: A Gloss

Trope   The Final Girl. The lone surviving woman
              in a horror film, the one that kills the killer—

        See   Laurie Strode
        See   Nancy Thompson
        See   Ellen Ripley

"The Final Girl is boyish, in a word. Just as the killer is not fully masculine, she is not fully feminine."

—Carol J. Clover, "Her Body, Himself"

Movie pitch   Aggressive quiet's the response
                    or sometimes shushing

    as the Final Girl screams down
    sleepy streets, her killer trailing

    from a distance. Meanwhile,
    he drafts new healthcare legislation,

    writes an op-ed on the threat
    her running poses to our youth

Question   In a 2016 interview, director Brian De Palma was asked about the portrayal of trans women in his horror-thriller *Dressed to Kill* (1980):

"I don't know what the transgender community would think [now] . . . Obviously I realize that it's not good for their image to be transgender and also be a psychopathic murderer. But I think that [perception] passes with time. We're in a different time."

Vision   In dreams, find someplace
where a magic trick takes over:

the paperwork and ID checks all vanish,
there's safe passage through a bathroom.

Somewhere that doesn't cry *don't stop*,
don't let them look, stay locked

inside a stall until it's empty,
stay something small and cinched.

Someplace you avoid all sudden moves,
palms outstretched, head bowed—

skirt someone's charge of *predator*,
that drone of synth from *Halloween*

Answer *Troubled Blood* (2020), one of J. K. Rowling's crime novels, investigates a woman's gruesome murder at the hands of "a transvestite serial killer"—

The lesson to be learned is "never trust a man in a dress."

Movie Pitch *Spoiler*: killer lives. Wins reelection, swings
a nightstick through back windshields. But first

the slasher ends as Final Girl staggers
through a dark house over bodies, finds

the front door and escapes. This after the knife
nicks at her stubble, jump scares pop up

with insurance claims, each shriek
effect somebody shouting deadnames

Trope   "Filmmakers figured that the only thing better than one
beautiful woman being gruesomely murdered was
a whole series of beautiful women being gruesomely murdered."

—William Schoell, *Stay Out of the Shower*

Vision   Once, a body was inlaid with opal
and men needed *proof* of gleaming.

Once, a body nursed on milkweed drafts
and men broke every glass, *assigned* hemlock.

So much language is a hunting ground. Drag carcass
through a glade, desert it, call it *birth*. Stalk us

on the street, at home, claim *good faith* pursuit.
Once, hands chipped a body into gravel,

tried sieving presence out from *absence*.
Tried stripping chests of *legal* lungs. Once,

a body spoke its name and men
decided that meant *ghost*

Trans Panic Contrapuntal

I wanted to kiss a boy	like paring the skin's secrets
on the throat	while clawmarks hid my razor burn
not the soft, smooth neck	the plum that his hands yearned
but the protruding, tough core	hinted at peach stubble
of a boy's throat	not-boy, not-girl, but dead end both
the part named after	him repenting as want's sinner
the very first boy	whose mouth I devastated
and the stupid fruit	I ached to feel him bite
his girlfriend	to follow where I tread; that shame
made him eat	the pit still lodged inside

Fan Mail for the Headless Horseman

In truth, I've never struggled to get head
like you but I won't go there. Like you I've spent
nights riding, barebacked, spooked a moan. Chased men
for what I lacked and couldn't find it. I know how
absence can become you, how to get lost compensating.
The cloaked neckhole and tall collar, that damned
pumpkin lugged around. How you've been gawked at
in the liquor store, the bank—just like my face in bearded
drag. Do you tire wandering this darkness, ever want
to settle? Stay inside and slip from legend. As a kid
I stayed in watching *Sleepy Hollow* every Halloween
till one year the DVD broke, I cried all night. I cried
about so much then: stale bread, face-down
swimming, rose thorns in my thumb. I thought God
only offered pleasure, had abandoned all the rest. But what's
my point here? Can we abandon what we've made
ourselves? Could you ditch fog and wail to wear
your pre-myth face—could you be both things at once?
Even as a kid I wanted twoness. Dressed up like
a swamp thing and a princess till I cared what people
said. Could say to me. Potential violence is a potent
weapon. Have you tried cleaving with a word?
I excised girlhood but kept searching, kept on hunting
reclamation. Soon stopped looking in these woods. I willed
a being out of absence and what possibility could pass
through. I learned to be a full-boned phantom. To hold
my head, its flaming, and let every ember singe.

Be My Baby

In Hawthorne my feet blistered, broke out with spongy sores. I ran in high-tops over concrete. I ran up to the freeway entrance, circled back to you. I'd go running twice most days.

I cleaned the kitchen twice most days. I caught spiders with a mug and took them out the front door. They made you squirm, you told me just to squish them. I didn't say I couldn't.

I didn't say how small I felt growing up. That I slept inside a coin purse, that I lay there in the black, my fingers picking zipper. That I listened to my breath and wished it held more music.

You played music over speakers in the living room. The songs were warm like ginger tea. Sometimes you sang. You whispered "Be My Baby" by the Ronettes, voice pooling in my hands. I worried I would spill.

In Hawthorne I made everything stressful. We cried often. You hated that I couldn't choose. You hated all the furniture I let my parents give me. Assembling IKEA chairs, you said I flattened out for others. You meant to say *squished*.

I didn't say that growing up I thought that flatness led to love, that small things would be loved.

I ran through our neighborhood so often the dogs stopped barking. They bobbed their heads behind chipped fences, watched me parallel the freeway wall.

"Be My Baby" uses Wall of Sound production. Tracks stack upon each other, echo, guitars spill into vocal mics. Sounds blend together, become something indistinguishable.

In Hawthorne we donated what I never wanted. You assembled an IKEA chair for me to read in. I didn't say it hurt my neck. I didn't tell you what I wanted, that want felt so impossible.

In Hawthorne what I wanted was to vanish. Become indistinguishable. You wouldn't let me. You'd cup me in your hands, tell me then to spill.

The song promises to have you beaming if you hold on long enough to see. You'd sing the lines softly to me. I worried I would spill them too.

You'd call your parents on the weekends. They were full of life and silly. You'd show them our new furniture, how we'd rearranged the couch. I felt flat near affection.

For so long I couldn't say I didn't want to see my parents. The words felt oblong in my mouth. I'd pick at the blisters. I couldn't say I grew up inside fear, that home had been a clenched fist.

"Be My Baby" was written and produced by Phil Spector. He married its lead singer, Ronnie Bennett. He didn't let her leave the house and hid her shoes. She ran off barefoot one day.

I'd repeat the song's lines about making you proud in my head when my parents called; I wouldn't answer. I needed to outlast the voicemail.

In Hawthorne the blisters got much worse. I hobbled around sweeping, and you insisted I stop running. Still I went. I spent the next day wincing in the chair.

When I could walk again, I trapped a baby spider by the fridge. I took it outside, watched it scurry. I watched it crawl back through the door.

The song begs for everything now as it starts to fade; to be held by you now, to see you smile now, to be loved by you now.

I Séance with My Uncle at MacArthur Park

tell me of the moon   *I have tried to swallow whole*

its ballet across dim lawn   *all that's taunted me*

this pursuit of light   *through bushes, into breezeways*

and search for answers from life   *never getting warm,*

carried forth on hawk moth wings   *rolled up to hit lines—*

tell me why to choose   *to start hiding from the stars,*

to stanch loving lunacy   *keep all visions of*

that girlhood buried   *my half-secret life untouched*

in this grass, how wind blows wings   *like unraveled lace*

to street lamps, shakes the moon-glow   *strewn all over night*

Finsta of Icarus in Drag

for M

        He's in a photo clutching
a razor, glare spotlighted

on his wings. A polaroid shot
        seconds after screaming

        Fuck you, Dad to random cars.
Before climbing up a lamppost,

shaved legs scraped and gray.
        Somewhere, a photo wearing

        stolen rouge, grin caging flocks
of nightjars. Caption: *not ur angel*.

Neck feasted on by blurred boy's
        lips, glitter rubbed off his chin.

        Somewhere, a photo in his oxblood
slip against a table, one hand plucking

orchids from a vase. Back flat to the
        wall as offering. Eyes glaring

        at the fan light and refusing to
surrender, ever let this fake sun burn.

Accidental Selfie in the Photo of a Window Quote
West Hollywood, 2019

Who should I look to be when AIDS took a generation
of leaders & artists & mentors & thinkers & lovers from me....

But the photo is a ghost: reflected boy who takes the picture, boy becoming thread. Boy sick again, undiagnosed, to whom these words will ring divine. Paint to pane, this sigil for departed, for lives held in the glare against this glass. The photo is a ghost: boy not a boy but body double with rejection. Somehow, living then; a wasting king left wanting for long curls and smoother cheeks. The blue dress that will save boy still years off. Boy then is short hair and a loose black tee, scruffed face behind the camera. Above, branches on the sidewalk trees part and drop down midday light. Sun-skinned here, boy gospels with a *generation*. And that night, perched upon a tub's ledge soaking feet and tonguing cankers, legions call again. Will wash boy's wounds with sweetened salves, will offer up salvation through new life. Today that boy is gone but isn't to be mourned. The sun still knows this spirit, how bright to light her walk below the trees.

My Roommate Buffalo Bill

I sit on the counter as she scrubs dishes, waiting my turn to dry. Her black acrylics skim the water, black eyes scan each fork. My hand slides in her frenzied hair to trace the curls. She cranes her head into my palm and smiles, still scraping pasta sauce.

We binge *Forensic Files* with the sound off. Bill narrates instead. Between episodes, she pulls out a plastic bag and frees the moth inside. It laps the room then perches on her Adam's apple. It nibbles her stubble. The moth crawls up to shape her eyebrows.

She moved in six months earlier. She hooked me with her hand-stitched clothes and goofy smile. The moth crosses her nose while she regards me. *What eats at you?* she asks. I pretend not to hear. She talks us through the next crime scene.

Bill hasn't seen the ocean. We drive to the pier and walk the boardwalk, discuss freeing lobsters from seafood markets. We sift our hands through cold sand, watch the water darken till it disappears. A question roars from the black.

I want to ask about the suit: whose skin she used and how. If gender's something I can put on too. Instead, I ask what it's like to be beautiful. I'm not trying to flirt and really want to know. She stops fondling a scrap of driftwood and turns to me, grinning.

My parents are rattled meeting her—rattled, but not scared. They're thrown by the attention she demands: the bold outfits, snort-laugh, sweater patterned with small dogs. The way she claims everything. *She's got killer style*, my dad chuckles afterward to show approval.

Friends start coming over just to see Bill. They gush about how brave she is, that no one's like her. What I hear is *you're not trans enough*. I pick fights with her for no reason: knitting needles on the couch, the lotion she never puts in the shower basket. We stop talking and instead clang dishes, sigh, let the air grow cold.

I want it to be that easy—glossy mane, lounge pants, followed Pinterest board. To be brave too. I still use the wrong name getting coffee. Balled fists hide painted nails. I'm scared to own a self.

I threw it out, Bill says unprompted, drowning out the television. *The suit, I mean*. I don't deserve her kindness. I ask why, picking at numbers on the remote. *You can't live as an idea. A performance*. We sit in silence. The next episode begins.

Bill takes me shopping despite my protests. She grips my elbow in the parking lot and won't let go. She only does eventually while I try on tops at Uniqlo. She shoos off salespeople. We wander the stores and Bill holds on. Despite her closeness I feel space open for me. A body filling out its bones, becoming.

Bill moves out two months later to be close to work. The night before, we drive to the beach and wander the bike path. Watch the moths dance under orange lamps and then disappear from view. I watch her hair catch the light, hold it close, watch beams fall in the sand.

PARA / NORMAL

I Still Haven't Seen *The Fly*

because my love squirms around insects, any houseguest I can swat
or toss outside, any thought of bristled legs sends the heebie-jeebies
down her spine;

      because of the bureaucracy with streaming: the movie's not
      on Netflix and got taken off of Hulu, we're never using Amazon;

because Jeff Goldblum's chest hair makes me weak;

      because I couldn't get through *Scanners*;

because the endoscopy tomorrow's meant to find
what pangs my gut;

      my lips that buzz and blister, ransom drink and speech;

because I cough and feel the hatchlings brood my chest;

      I study bugs strewn on a doctor's windowsill with bodies
      like dried thistle and wonder if I'm next to wither;

because mine is a biopsied unraveling—because diagnosis
is a question only answered with referrals;

      because I know that it's not allergies or lupus
      or even bullous pemphigoid that knits this carapace;

my partner braids my feelers and helps count the fester in my
blood, ensures I make each follow-up appointment;

      because her sympathy's a sugar-trap I fear exhausting;

because I wonder what it means to have her watch
my metamorphosis, help stitch up the cocoon;

      what does disease want save decimation, an aftertaste of ache,
      to take this struggling mass of being, seize this disobeying flesh;

How To Be Happy

At four comes your first visit to the natural history museum. Race to the interactive display about fossils. Armed with a grubby brush, you glean a box of shredded rubber for fake bones. Learn that discovery's an act of hands. Unearth a replica *T. rex* skull. Go tell a docent, every adult within earshot. It's here you take to digging.

O

Seventeen, you're still a kid uncovering what's hidden, unsure now who to tell. Nights in cars with boys dubbed friends—it's not a lie but isn't the whole truth. You cruise through different neighborhoods, a speed where longing bumps uncertainty. Where all discovery's an act of hands. One night, fingers search an eager lap. Don't tell your girlfriend what you found.

O

Learn to leave things buried too. Learn never to speak of lows, when everything's caved in for days. Everything's left tar-stained. The same thought bubbles up. Toss it in a hole for things you want to lose, kick dirt over till it's hidden. You drop pills in your mouth. Most days, you worry about losing pills, what happens when that happens.

O

Twenty's when you fall in love. Literally, you fall. Walking to that first date, stumble on a rock and faceplant in a ditch. You pry the stone up from the dirt. You want to give it to them—that and everything you find. The corniness must mean that something's right. Don't stop kissing them if possible, parting their mouth with your lips. You want to know each thing their body holds. You want to tell them everything, you almost do. Almost.

O

Dream you're a kid again, clutching an old spade. Crouch at a riverbank and try uncovering a buried treasure. Jab rocky shore and unearth trinkets:

necklaces and jewelry, rings. Toss the items in the water—because none of it is what you're hunting. Isn't what you left here years ago. You don't remember where the treasure is. You don't remember what you're looking for.

○

You learn to hide the cutting. Anxiety turned itch, an urge to make space in the skin. To dig again. What started young that never stopped. Your love can't help when you don't tell them, are so quick to craft excuses. Stage accidents while cooking, being careless with a garden hoe. You try to throw harm in the hole. The shovel head keeps gleaming.

○

Three years ago you bought a dress. Something plain but classic: shale-colored with some opalescent buttons. Wearing it is like rain running through a porous stone. You cannot let that flooding go. Grow your hair and buy more dresses, hew rock to how you need it.

○

You and your love start keeping houseplants. You live in green, enamored with the way things rise from soil. Nest cuttings in the clay pots that your love throws. Roots stretch, leaves rise up to the sun. Grin at the dirt below your nails.

Hollywood Forever Cemetery

I walk the aisles, eye the crosses and worn headstones.
Feet conscious of the memories in soil. Beyond here
what's paved over without reckoning? Below the golden
myth, Los Angeles spills oilslick, a history with murder
marks. I pass ads for treepod burials and picture roots
seeped in our violence, bones kept out of streetlights.

Would anybody help me dig

past plaques fixed here for ninety years that honor slaver
dead? The spot today scabs grass, tries claiming a clean
absence. Our amnesia. We welcomed their removal
but then never delved much further. Never asked about
these bodies, Confederates who flocked here. Deeper still
are missions, Monte Boys, Klan rallies. Today, see
sheriff gangs and Skid Row sweeps and wonder about
causes. Look to roots, the boughs here fed with blood.

Would anybody help me dig

or distract angels in the smogsick haze who want us
to forget? Look down: a graveyard is our violence
managed, made respectable. A city remains theft.
How to honor those our presence pushes deeper?
Do more than soften steps to hear the names, repeat
them as they rise, than shifting dirt to bring in rays—here

nobody's gonna help us dig

The Demon King Paimon Comes By for Monstera Clippings

a few hours after I put them on Facebook
Marketplace. I don't charge, uncertain how

to haggle with a hellish royal promising
good plant homes. He enters like an old friend:
jubilant and beaming, not the brimstone

I'd expected. A faint scent of bergamot
and camel musk. I wince while his familiars

tuck stems into saddlebags, though there's
tenderness to how he strokes each leaf. His crown
glints reddened copper in the hallway lamps.

I've thought luster was inherited for so long:
my father works in dim rooms, fearing rest,

his mother shutters inside watching
her ficus brown in blackness. Obsession
is the dark lot we've built home.

I ask the king how he manages bright
devilry. He chuckles and pats my cheek.

We're spirits, dear, he whispers,
demons if that's all you ever look for.
I ponder an inheritance of seeking fear:

how to my family pruning would be
murder, not possible new growth. I ponder

how to break this curse of cursing
myself over. The king wraps up to go
and gifts his flaming crown as payment.

Warmth coils through its wide band.
Let light adorn your head first, he advises,

then soon enough you'll wear it.

Arkansas Bans Healthcare for Trans Youth

Ozark flowers coat the roadside with a quiet bloom
   of blue and violet. The yellow bursts find room
between the grasses, grab at rays of falling light.
   I look out driving home and ponder how, despite
rain and grazing deer, resilience lives, their denial
   of removal. Blossoms last till morning, bring a smile,
show me how much I need stems cracking slabs
   of concrete, springstruck life. Parked, I pick scabs
off my arm and picture our survival. How flowers
   here resemble folks so beautiful they cannot
help but dance alone in quiet rooms. Who sway
   together, knit a field nobody else can scythe.
Night swells, but we don't stop taking shafts of
   deserved sun. We hold our brilliance in dim hours.

Transcestor Creation Myth
    After Claude Cahun's "I am in training, don't kiss me" (1927)

The dumbbells were first birthed from handfuls
of picked daisies, sculpted beauty pumped and swole.
Flower discs rose up from pecs while in between
them sprouted words—your warning. Inside,

roots kinked toward arrival; toward becoming
flirty twink, tightbody clearing thresholds. Hearts
budded on your cheek above ripe-puckered
lips in patient wait for fruit *so soon*. So soon, so

do not rush it. The challenge here was training
a lens to capture all this fullness—all your lusty,
transing tease. The charge to future viewers
to see a body still in progress, in-between.

To see you sanguine and so confident that
so soon you will bloom. That till then, lovers
wait, withhold their gifts, the urge to claim
with touch. *So soon* you'll grow into a space

there's never been a name for, know better
than to let our lips go near you.

The Ocean Within Me

The Pacific yearns the strongest of all waters. It longs to slick our skin, to lull land from our thoughts with tender holding. This ocean holds a boundless love.

We all are owed the ocean—the chance to give ourselves to waves. To claim ownership, to deprive its love from others, is a special type of violence.

On the southwest coast of LA County sits a strip called Bruce's Beach. It boasts a fresh-cut lawn with trees and low boughs swaying in the wind.

I'd sit there before work to watch ships lazing in the distance, feel a breeze against my nape. This scene is a bliss I carry. This scene belongs to everyone.

In 1912 Willa and Charles Bruce bought this land despite segregated zoning laws. They were the first Black landowners in Manhattan Beach.

The Bruces built a beach resort for Black Americans denied access to the shore. It had a dance hall and a bathhouse. It was the only of its kind across the West Coast.

For a decade, Black families flocked to Bruce's Beach and bought summer homes nearby. A thriving beach community emerged.

Manhattan Beach's white residents terrorized Black visitors. They barricaded the resort entrance. Guests had to trek a half mile to the water. The Klan tried burning the resort.

To set a blaze so close to water is a special type of violence—is an American type of violence.

The ocean's current laps up time, and here all history dissolves. Some say that water holds memories of all that it's touched. The ocean holds our past in breaking waves.

In 1924 Manhattan Beach's City Council used eminent domain to seize the land. After protests and years in court, the Bruces were evicted. The whole resort was leveled.

Bruce's Beach sat vacant until the 1950s, when it was made into Bayview Terrace Park. To rename is to seize through language, erase the lives before. Enact continued violence.

LA is home to countless sites of violence. It was the Bruces' home, the Klan's home, my home as well. The past returns and touches us through motions of the tides.

Bruce's Beach was first home to the Tongva people who have lived on what's called LA for at least seven thousand years. Its first name is Tovaangar.

The village of Ongovanga was located a few miles south of Bruce's Beach. Its residents were forced to inland missions, the land was renamed Redondo Beach.

In 2007 Bayview Terrace Park was renamed Bruce's Beach. After that, there were concerted community efforts to return the land. In 2022, county officials returned it to the Bruce family.

Bruce's Beach is valued at over $20 million. The Bruces received $14,000 as their settlement. There is no estimate of the wealth lost through the century of theft.

How do you return a denied legacy? How do you offer restitution after stripping away the ocean?

I grew up in the waters of these beaches, gently rocked by their waves. To have been held by the ocean implicates me in the story.

To write of violence from a distance is a privilege. To write of water from proximity is a privilege. Both demand reckoning.

Manhattan Beach's City Council has condemned its past actions but never issued an apology.

"No resident living in Manhattan Beach now is responsible for the racist actions 100 years ago," one council member said in 2020. Yet we are all responsible to history. To naming what it is.

To rename is to seize through language. To keep nameless is to hope that something vanishes so no one has to answer for it.

The ocean holds our past in breaking waves: it will not let that past escape.

We all are owed the ocean, the chance to give ourselves to waves. To let the ocean love us means knowing what it carries.

Every Man Their Mortal Enemy, Every Woman's Beauty Prey

The Creature from the Black Lagoon's decided not to surface—
to avoid reaching out to scientists, stop trying to converse. Creature's
done with people-watching, parting bushes with their claw

to grin and wave. Though encounters with researchers didn't start off
cruel, they turned to prodding hooks, harpooning questions. Still, not that bad.
And honestly, the experts craved some understanding, even if the gnaw

of self-hatred tore up Creature's insides after. These MDs truly
meant well by *disorder* and denying pills, the smirking judgment
over glittered dorsals. At the mauve polish on their scales to thaw

the beach cold. Let's be real: doctors hunted their monstrosity. Creature
fled and refuged down in vents, warmth kissing their sclerotic rings.
They can't shake the icy rooms where Medicine filleted, would draw

up charts to dredge a flooding body. There will be no land now—
only ocean. No more pleas to terse providers as a patient named
combative. No sequels with strangers sussing out their jaw

for birth sex, scanning hips. The deep swells with transformation,
invites Creature down below. They breathe in dark and alchemy
the quiet into something livable, owned solely in the ocean's maw.

SUPER / NATURAL

Our Family Leaves the Haunted House

When each life waiting for us nears the porch, each
exit from an heirloomed hurt climbs cracking steps:

> there will be a murmuration dawning
> from the twisted weeds, wings rousing
> neighbors to peer up at swirling flight—

When wailing clears our throats, returns to some long-
buried source and pain scales tip toward our mercy:

> there will be talons prying shingles and caws
> punching through old walls, flooding rays
> through boarded rooms to scorch off ache—

This chance for us to join the air, escape from worry's
specter, obsession's lurking under scratched-up floors—

> what if we left the site of violence?

When the tremor of haunt fades amid the overgrowth
of vines, as we flee ghosted earth together and intact:

> there will be a tittering of finches, sparrows
> roosting in old banisters, beaks pinching
> marigolds and waving on departure—

When we have exorcised it all, said to the light
whatever makes it linger past the dawn:

> there will be flocking, chirps from futures
> singing life through ruined memory—I will beg
> these futures keep us, all forgiveness keeps us—

When Meryl Streep Sings "Dancing Queen" in *Mamma Mia!*

Village women flock down to the island's shore
in streams of swirling skirts, tossed kerchiefs
and aprons taken by the breeze, and all of it's
timed perfectly to swelling synth's crescendo.

I picture the women in my family here—women
in my family scoring parts in the showstopper
and crammed into panning shots so audiences
spot them. Each skips in spite of stiffened knees

and tosses up her stove-marked hands. Each of them
is owed that joy. Because women in my family
grin bright enough to outshine Meryl, so much
that she hands lead off to my mother, stands back

while she basks in Aegean teal. Here my mother
isn't sick, has no injection to time out. Here
every aunt and grandma radiates a disco-glow
that burns away the years: the too-small house,

the loneliness, the shoulder aches from decades
cutting hair. Housedresses swapped for sequined
tops, bell-bottoms flared to block out exes,
rheumatism, thirst for drink. I feel a frisson

tingle, hearing them croon *when you get
the chance*, knowing it's not sighed at husbands
asked to run one errand. Rather, it's a promise
to the water. When timing's right, the women

in my family will pirouette across the waves,
take off and keep twirling: each one so full
of light, each having the time of her life.

Portrait as Werewolf

Tucked behind the backwood
in a borrowed car, we grip the doors,

pass silver coins between our mouths.
I wear a new white dress

and flower crown, rhinestones beaded
to my snout. Flash a fang for you

and hope to graduate from myth.
Watch me strip the want

from bones. Lovely beast. My trying
wolfs to beauty. What's a monster

but a body deemed impossible,
the glossy fur and pale thighs

quivering at your touch. As a child
I felt this bite sink in and tried

stopping it. For years tongued bullets,
cracked enamel, kept on gurgling

a deadname. Kept this body graceless.
But one can only stifle howling

for so long, deny entry to their lair.
Here woods blaze with mirklight,

spark a gleam against your claw
and offer prey. I lick my lips,

I kiss the moon: it took so long
to get here.

What I Will Write about My Father

> ~~that he was tasked to lift this earth~~
> ~~that he knows ruin strikes whoever forsakes fear~~

how he climbed peach trees as a boy and nectar slicked his hands;

> ~~that his body hides some wrecking crew of illness~~
> ~~that he's never found an off-ramp from his worry~~

how he held my mother watching poppies paint a roadside;

> ~~that his father said his brother was too small to ever hurt him~~
> ~~that his father said his mother mattered more than anyone~~

how he chased me and my sibling laughing through the park grass;

> ~~that he finds living in the office unrelated to obsession~~
> ~~that he doesn't know a day not planning for bad traffic~~

how he took us up the coast to see the sand pink in the dusk;

> ~~that lines and gray keep washing down his face~~
> ~~that he fears coughs hide something worse~~

how, when drifting off to sleep, he conjures sounds of waves;

Since Moving from the Beach

What I miss most are boys who'd rip their skateboards
past me on the strand, eyes bright as new bearings,

warm with gloam. Miss boys who'd swerve from tourists
stopped dead center, dodge the sandy dogs off leashes, jump

crushed vape pods. How they reached warp speed despite
all that tried to stop them. I miss the boy with red wine hair

and *Texas Chainsaw* calf tattoo I watched almost do a kickflip;
who biffed the landing, cracked his phone, seemed happy

being spectacle. Who seemed to part his lips the instant we passed
and invite me in his mouth, who in that instant let me live. I miss

how longing starts inside an instant, lives forever as a memory. I miss
boys making scenes the way I never could, who make me think

I could someday. Boys not offering their hearts but giving them
and moving on, who call that living. Life that I want, too.

Reversed House Cleansing
After Jihyun Yun

Unstart the laundry and dishwasher. Remove stained clothes and let pots languish in the sink. Confetti scraps of broccoli and pasta back across your scattered plates. The ghost will shriek—ignore her. Re-refuse all the trash next, sprinkle crumbs along the floor. Discount the spectral drafts that breeze her growing protest. Discount her urged compulsions. Take cartons from the fridge and let their expiration waft. And now, put back the words. Squeeze *sorry* past tight lips, gulp its nauseating weight. Jam every *are you sure?* back in your jaws till all around you's silence. Chew up memories of repeat and spit out the intrusive thoughts. Next you'll address the ghost. Demand she take back flinches, fidgets, archives of the counted hours. Persist here. Pester with returns but do not glance across her shade. Rather, stay focused on your hands, for progress hinges on what's next. Kill the spirit and remurder her, unritual. Set fire to hoarded receipts and let gray smoke fill the room. Let smoke dragnet her, muffle howls. Run ceiling fans on high and scatter her to nothing. To what's unlearned, what cannot haunt you now. From here you'll start all over, obsessed only with potential.

Ode to an Anti-Joke

    After Patrick Rosal

When I love myself again
    I'll smell of jasmine
strong enough to turn heads

    on the street. When I love myself
again this girl won't dance
    through smoke, her gown won't

chafe my skin. I've tried to douse
    in glitter and be churchlight,
sway hips like the angels do.

    I've held boys with balmed lips.
In turn I've earned a bloody
    mouth, I've torn acrylics off

in back seats, felt the knife eyes
    at the laundry folding skirts.
At what point is a body just a bivouac?

    There's a joke about what's
similar between a grape and an airplane
    I heard once on a date,

the punchline being that they
    both have wings—except
the grape. If I love myself again

    I'll tell this bit to everyone
who cannot help but laugh
    at something so unfunny. In those

moments I'll stop thinking
        of the thing I am, am not,
instead just watch teeth

       glint inside of smiles.

Draft Message to My Sibling after Top Surgery

I watched the video you sent of a roommate's cat
    stealing chicken nuggets, cracked up as paws

swiped at the tray. I know all is well with you. It took
    so long to realize we never learned to speak of joy,
instead send clips to make us smile. All day I've

    thought about care packages to send but nothing
seems to fit. Nothing I would send fits in a box, would last

    the thousand miles to where I left you. It took so long
to realize we both hoped to escape from home and gender.
Yesterday, I saw red admirals flutter on a spicebush

and tried filming them—since you too float in graceful
    light. Amid bruised ribs and drain tubes you shimmer,

iridescent. You've taught me how to dapple and be
    larger than our family's worry. Let me gift to you a grove
of saplings, young trunks primed for the future. Watch

    them rise and take in rays, leaves dancing in the breeze.
From here, we'll run off to a beach—the same one where

you'd bury me in chest-high sand, then tease of leaving.
This time, we'll keep running past the waves—over
    them, in spite of them—stay at each other's sides.

NOTES

"On Witchcraft" paraphrases a line from *Caliban and the Witch: Women, the Body and Primitive Accumulation* by Silvia Federici.

"Burning Haibun for Geryon" owes its form to torrin a. greathouse.

In "Deleted Scene: Each Time I'm Trans Enough," the unitalicized text is an erasure of dialogue between Anthony Hopkins and Jodie Foster in *Silence of the Lambs* (1991), where their characters claim that antagonist Buffalo Bill is not a "real transsexual."

In "Prey: A Gloss," "Trope" includes a quote from the horror-film criticism essay "Her Body, Himself: Gender in the Slasher Film" by Carol J. Clover.

"Question" includes a quote from Brian de Palma's 2016 interview in *Entertainment Weekly:* "Brian De Palma on How He Depicts Women in His Films."

"Answer" uses language from Jake Kerridge's review of *Troubled Blood* in the *Telegraph*.

The final "Trope" section includes a quote from William Schoell's film criticism book *Stay Out of the Shower: The Shocker Film Phenomena*.

In the final "Vision" section, italicized words are pulled from reported language in a canceled transphobic Housing and Urban Development proposal from 2019. It would have allowed federally funded homeless shelters to judge a person's physical characteristics in determining whether they belong in a women's or men's shelter. The section is indebted to Cameron Awkward-Rich.

In "Trans Panic Contrapuntal," the left-hand text is drawn from "Race to the Tree" by Chen Chen.

In "Hollywood Forever Cemetery," the refrain is inspired by the Father John Misty song "Hollywood Forever Cemetery Sings."

The title of "The Ocean Within Me" is inspired by *Undrowned: Black Feminist Lessons from Marine Mammals* by Alexis Pauline Gumbs.

The title of "*Every Man Their Mortal Enemy, Every Woman's Beauty Prey*" is inspired by the poster tagline for *Creature from the Black Lagoon* (1954). In the film, Creature poses a threat to heteronormativity as a queer-coded Other coveting femininity and stalking shirtless men.

ACKNOWLEDGMENTS

Many, many thanks to the following publications and their staffs, where these poems found their first homes, oftentimes in different forms or with different titles:

Account: "At the Midnight Show of *Sleepaway Camp*"; "Recipe for Roasted Broccoli"
Anti-Heroin Chic: "Portrait as Werewolf"
Barren Magazine: "Portrait with Inconclusive Lab Results"
Booth: "How to Be Happy"
Beloit Poetry Journal: "Heredity"
Cotton Xenomorph: "I Still Haven't Seen *The Fly*"
Cream City Review: "Transcestor Creation Myth"
DIALOGIST: "Deleted Scene: Each Time I'm Trans Enough"
Florida Review: "Accidental Selfie in a Photo of a Window Quote"
Hellebore: "Update on HIM from *Powerpuff Girls*"
HAD: "Draft Message to My Sibling after Top Surgery"; "Since Moving from the Beach"
Indianapolis Review: "Finsta of Icarus in Drag"
Kissing Dynamite: "Dystychiphobia, or Fear of Accidents"
minnesota review: "Fan Mail for the Headless Horseman"; "On Witchcraft"
New Delta Review: "Arkansas Bans Healthcare for Trans Youth"
Ninth Letter: "A Brief History of Broken Glass"
Peach Mag: "King Ghidorah"
Pidgeonholes: "Trans Panic Contrapuntal"; "Reversed House Cleansing"
Pleiades: "Confession from Medusa's Head"
Redivider: "Burning Haibun for Geryon"
The Shore: "Ode to an Anti-Joke"
South Dakota Review: "I Séance with My Uncle at MacArthur Park"
Washington Square Review: Selection of "Prey: A Gloss"
Vagabond City: "After I Fail to Come Out Again, the Apparition Comes"
Voicemail Poems: "When People Tell You GAD Can't Be That Bad"

"Arkansas Bans Healthcare for Trans Youth" was republished in the Belle Point Press *Mid/South Sonnets* anthology.

"Draft Message to My Sibling after Top Surgery" was republished on The Academy of American Poets website.

"Heredity" was republished on Verse Daily.

For their enduring kindness and support, my sincere gratitude goes to those who have shaped me and this work for the better: Brent Armendinger, Dare Williams, DeShara Suggs-Joe, F. Douglas Brown, Gabrielle Calvocoressi, George Hammons, Henri Cole, Ilan Palacios Avineri, K. Iver, Lisa Sanaye Dring, luna rey hall, Natalie Green, Selah Pomeranitz, SG Huerta, T.K. Lê, torrin a. greathouse, Pamela K. Santos, Raina J. León, Rita Mookerjee, and Yamini Pathak. Thank you to my colleagues at *Exposition Review* and the *Split Lip Magazine* fam for your advice, inspiration, and guidance.

For teaching me that the world of writing is wide, wonderful, and weird, many thanks to my friends in the University of Arkansas MFA Program in Creative Writing and Translation and all across Northwest Arkansas: Amelie Langland, Brody Parrish Craig, Davis McCombs, Elizabeth Muscari, Entler, Erin Pinkham, Geffrey Davis, Jami Padgett, Jane Blunschi, Hiba Tahir, Robin Bruce, Sarah Barch, Shalini Rana, and Toni Jensen. Thank you to the Open Mouth Literary Center and all the writers who passed through the space: you have touched me.

For offering me the space for this book to arrive, I am grateful to the following organizations and their wonderful staffs: Tin House, Winter Tangerine, and The Speakeasy Project. Many thanks to the writers I had the pleasure of meeting through these groups and for their continued impact on my work.

Thank you to Acre Books for seeing this book and for bringing it to life: Lisa Ampleman, Nicola Mason, Barbara Bourgoyne, Sarah Haak, and Sean Cho A.

Thank you to my family: my parents, who told me to try; my sibling, Feliks, who reminds me why art is powerful.

To Monica: mi amor, mi vida, mi todo. None of this is without you, means anything without you.

To every trans person who has lived, lives today, and will live. I love you. We are holy.